THE SECOND WORLD WAR IN THE AIR IN PHOTOGRAPHS

1943

L. ARCHARD

AMBERLEY

First published 2015

Amberley Publishing
The Hill, Stroud
Gloucestershire, GL5 4EP

www.amberley-books.com

British Library Cataloguing in Publication Data.
A catalogue record for this book is available from the British Library.

ISBN 978 1 4456 2248 4 (print)
ISBN 978 1 4456 2271 2 (ebook)

Typesetting and Origination by Amberley Publishing.
Printed in Great Britain.

Contents

Introduction

In terms of the war in the air, 1943 would be a major year for significant bomber operations. Perhaps the two most famous, for the British and Americans respectively, were the Dambusters raid in mid-May and the Ploesti raid at the beginning of August. However, there were also the Eighth Air Force's raids against Regensburg and Schweinfurt, the joint Operation Gomorrah targeting Hamburg, and the RAF's concerted campaigns against the industrial facilities of the Ruhr valley, and against Berlin.

The bomber campaign in 1943 started in January with two two-night attacks on Berlin by RAF Bomber Command, and by the first all-American air raid launched by the Eighth Air Force against Germany, in which the target was the German North Sea naval base of Wilhelmshaven. On the Eastern Front, Soviet forces captured the last airfield in Stalingrad, meaning that the Luftwaffe could no longer supply the besieged Sixth Army by air. The Sixth Army's commander, Field Marshal Paulus, would surrender to the Soviets at the end of the month.

In the Far East, February saw the start of the first mission for Orde Wingate's Chindits, an incursion from India into Japanese-occupied Burma inspired by the tactics the Japanese themselves had used. The Chindits would move on foot through the jungle, using the element of surprise to target Japanese lines of communications, such as roads and railways. They would rely on aircraft to both drop supplies by parachute and act as close air support. February marked the start of the first of the year's major RAF bombing campaigns when Bomber Command attacked the industrial city of Essen; this was the beginning of a four-month campaign of air raids against the Ruhr valley. Essen, the home of the famous Krupp works, would be hit particularly hard during the next few months.

In March, increased activity by U-boats in the mid-Atlantic, insufficiently covered by aircraft, led to devastating losses among convoys. B-24 Liberator bombers, very effective as anti-submarine patrol aircraft because of their long range, had been in use in this role since 1941, at first by the RAF from bases in Scotland, Northern Ireland and then Iceland, and later by the US Navy and the RCAF from the west as well. However, it was an increase in the number of Liberators made available for anti-submarine patrols in April and May 1943 following the toll taken on shipping in March that started to turn the tide. An effective new base would come into use in 1943 as Portugal gave permission for Allied air and naval forces to use the Azores islands, 850 miles into the Atlantic from the Iberian Peninsula, as a base. Interestingly, when the Portuguese government agreed to this in August, they cited the Anglo-Portuguese Treaty of 1373.

April saw another blow to Japanese forces when Admiral Isoroku Yamamoto, the Commander-in-Chief of the Imperial Japanese Navy and one of its most significant strategists who had conceived the idea of striking a decisive blow against the Americans, which led to the Pearl Harbor attack, was killed. In April 1943, Yamamoto set out on a tour of inspection of Japanese bases in the South Pacific. US Navy code-breakers deciphered a message containing details of Yamamoto's itinerary, and a squadron of P-38 Lightning long-range fighters were detailed to intercept his flight on 18 April as he flew between Rabaul on New Britain and the island of Bougainville in the Solomon Islands.

In the Mediterranean, the Luftwaffe sent transport aircraft from Italy to Tunisia to airlift out German troops who had been isolated by the Allied forces as they advanced towards Tunis, and, in what became known as the Palm Sunday Massacre, on 18 April a force of sixty-five Ju 52s carrying German troops evacuated from Tunisia, escorted by sixteen Axis fighters and five Bf 110s, was intercepted by a mixed force of RAF Spitfires and USAAF P-40 Thunderbolts. In the ensuing battle, twenty-four Junkers were shot down, along with ten of their escorts, and a further thirty-five were damaged but managed to crash-land in Sicily. The heavy losses sustained by the Luftwaffe in its attempts to maintain communications with German forces in North Africa and in the operation to supply the Sixth Army in Stalingrad would cripple its transport force.

In the meantime, the bombing of German cities continued. In mid-April, there was a heavy RAF raid on Stuttgart, while in May the campaign against the Ruhr continued with a raid on the city of Wuppertal that caused heavy civilian casualties. Perhaps the most spectacular attempt to cripple industrial production in the Ruhr, however, came with the famous Dambusters raid, properly Operation Chastise, carried out on the night of 16/17 May. Using special bouncing bombs, code-named Upkeep, developed by aircraft designer and engineer Barnes Wallis (who had designed the versatile Wellington bomber for Vickers), a special squadron of Bomber Command under Wing Commander Guy Gibson attacked the Möhne, Eder and Sorpe dams using Lancaster bombers modified to be able to carry the Upkeep bombs, successfully breaching the Möhne and Eder. The raid was a great propaganda success for the RAF and of course inspired the film *The Dam Busters*, starring Richard Todd and Michael Redgrave. Of the nineteen Lancaster bombers involved in the raid, eight failed to return – almost 40 per cent of the force. The Germans estimated some 1,600 people had died as a result of dams being breached, including French, Belgian, Dutch and Ukrainian prisoners and labourers. Although the raid had a real effect, particularly on electricity production in the Ruhr, it was at best a minor inconvenience to the Germans; the greatest effect was on British morale. 617 Squadron was kept in existence to carry out further raids against special targets requiring pinpoint accuracy. More conventional bombing raids against the Ruhr continued through to the end of June, leading to the evacuation of many German civilians out of the area.

As well as the bombing of Germany, a campaign of bombing had begun against Italy, particularly the islands of Sicily and Sardinia, both potential landing grounds for Allied troops following the end of the North African campaign with the surrender of German and Italian forces there on 13 May. This bombing continued through June and into July, including attacks on Naples and on the islands of Pantelleria and Lampedusa, roughly between Tunisia and Sicily, which surrendered to Allied forces on 11 and 12 June respectively. On 10 July, Operation Husky, the invasion of Sicily, began. The first wave of the invasion involved the use of British and American airborne troops. The British paratroopers, men of the 1st Airborne Division, had already seen fighting in North Africa, fighting their German counterparts, the Fallschirmjäger. They would face the German paratroopers on Sicily as well. The Allied force was a combination of parachutists and glider-borne infantry intended to seize bridges needed by the seaborne invasion forces and to land inland as well. However, high winds meant that many of the airborne forces were scattered across the island, some of the gliders landing in the sea as well. Allied aircraft based across the Mediterranean in North Africa provided close air support for the troops on the ground, and disrupted the movements and supply lines of the defending German and Italian forces. As part of the increased air activity over Italy, Rome was bombed for the first time by the Allies when American bombers attacked a railway marshalling yard and various government ministries in the city centre.

In another significant move, in July Hitler was briefed on the V2 rocket programme and approved top priority for the project. At the same time, the RAF launched a series of attacks aimed against the German V-weapon programme in July and August, bombing the research facility at Peenemünde on the Baltic coast, among other sites. At the end of July, Operation Gomorrah, a sustained bombing campaign against the port of Hamburg, was launched; at the time it was the heaviest assault in aviation history. The city was bombed by the RAF and USAAF for eight days and seven nights from 24 July. The attack on the night of 27/28 July was especially severe, with unusually warm and dry weather helping to lead to a firestorm that destroyed about 8 square miles of the city. Hamburg's labour force was permanently reduced by a tenth while the city's industry production never recovered. Operation Gomorrah shook the German leadership; Hitler is reported to have said that more raids of such a weight would force Germany out of the war.

August in the air war was dominated by two missions carried out by the USAAF. At the start of the month, B-24 Liberators of the US Eighth and Ninth air forces flying from airfields in North Africa carried out a raid against the Romanian oil refineries gathered around the city of Ploesti. A force of 177 bombers took off from airfields around Benghazi, Libya, flying across the Adriatic and over Albania and Yugoslavia, into Romania to attack the seven refineries, attacking at a very low level to try to evade the German defences. However, the raid was costly, becoming known as Black Sunday, as fifty-three of the B-24s failed to return. Although after the raid it was estimated that production had been reduced by 40 per cent, most of the damage to the refineries was repaired within weeks. Later in the month, a force of B-17s of the Eighth Air Force, escorted by Spitfires and P-47 Thunderbolts, launched simultaneous attacks on the Messerschmitt assembly plant at Regensburg, one of two locations in which the production of Bf 109 fighters was concentrated (the other being Wiener Neustadt, just outside Vienna), and the ball-bearing factories at Schweinfurt. Regensburg, in the south-east of Bavaria, was far enough from the Eighth Air Force's bases in East Anglia that the bombers could not return there – they landed at airfields in North Africa instead. Of the 146 bombers that set off for Regensburg, 122 successfully landed in Tunisia. Casualties on the Schweinfurt raid were thirty-six of the 230 aircraft that set off.

By 17 August, the whole of Sicily was under Allied control. On 3 August, the Italian government signed a secret armistice with the Allies. Mussolini had been ousted from power on 25 July; he had lost what was effectively a vote of confidence at a meeting of the Grand Council of Fascism the day before, and King Victor Emmanuel III, who had been planning to oust Mussolini himself as the war went increasingly badly for Italy, replaced the prime minister with Marshal Badoglio, formerly Chief of the General Staff. Mussolini was arrested by the *carabinieri* and held under arrest in various locations around Italy before being moved to the mountaintop Hotel Campo Imperatore in the Abruzzo. However, Hitler had not forgotten his old friend, and on 12 September a force of German Fallschirmjäger along with SS troops under the command of Otto Skorzeny landed by glider on the mountain where the hotel is located and overwhelmed Mussolini's 200 *carabinieri* guards. Mussolini was flown off the mountain in a Fiesler Storch light aircraft along with Skorzeny, and taken via Rome to Vienna. In the meantime, British forces had landed on the mainland of Italy at Reggio Calabria on 3 September, the secret Italian armistice had been made public by the Allies on 8 September and the Germans, who had been expecting something of this nature to happen, disarmed their former allies and prepared to carry on the fight without them. On 9 September, Allied forces made another landing on mainland Italy, at Salerno.

On 4 September, an airborne operation in New Guinea led to the occupation of Nadzab airfield outside Lae by the 503rd Parachute Regiment. General MacArthur watched the battle from a B-17 Flying Fortress circling overhead. The attack on Nadzab has been described as the textbook airborne attack of the Second World War and persuaded the Japanese commanders that their positions in the south-west Pacific were overextended.

In October, the Eighth Air Force made another visit to the ball-bearing plants at Schweinfurt, targeted because ball bearings were vital parts for all sorts of machinery important for the German war effort, and their production in Germany was concentrated around Schweinfurt. Of the 291 Flying Fortresses that set off for Schweinfurt on 14 October, sixty failed to return, another seventeen were too badly damaged to be repaired and a further 121 had varying degrees of damage. The casualties were heavy because bad weather meant that the bomb groups were spread out and vulnerable to the German fighters and flak; although there were escort fighters, P-47 Thunderbolts, they were not carrying drop tanks, which limited their range. As a result of the second Schweinfurt raid, daylight bomber raids over Germany were suspended until P-51 Mustangs were available to act as escort fighters, as their long range meant that they could accompany the bombers all the way to the target.

November saw the start of a concerted RAF bombing campaign, known as the Battle of Berlin, against the German capital. The battle started with a raid on the night of

18/19 November, which caused only light damage to Berlin as the city was covered by cloud. However, the next raid, which came on the night of 22/23 November, was the most effective one carried out against Berlin by the RAF during the war. Dry weather conditions meant that several firestorms were created and heavy damage caused to the residential districts of Tiergarten, Charlottenburg, Schöneberg and Spandau to the west of Berlin. Among the notable buildings damaged or destroyed were the Deutsche Opernhaus on Charlottenburg's Bismarckstrasse and the Kaiser Wilhelm Memorial Church on the Kurfürstendamm, which is preserved today and serves as a memorial.

In December, the Luftwaffe carried out an air raid on Bari, on the Adriatic coast of southern Italy. A force of 105 Junkers Ju 88s of Luftflotte 2 achieved complete surprise, sinking twenty-eight ships in Bari harbour. One of these ships was the SS *John Harvey*, which was carrying a cargo of mustard gas bombs apparently sent to Italy to be used in retaliation if the Germans used chemical weapons there, as they had threatened to do. Eighty-three military personnel died from the effects of the gas; in total, 1,000 military personnel and sailors and about 1,000 civilians died. This raid proved that although the Germans were on the back foot and had taken heavy losses, they were still a force to be reckoned with, something that would be proved still further in the years to come; in October 1943, an order had been placed for the construction of 12,000 V-2 rockets. Launch sites were also discovered to be under production for the V-1.

However, in November, at the Tehran Conference, Roosevelt, Churchill and Stalin had reached an agreement about the invasion of France by the western Allies in June 1944. Although the Germans could not yet be counted out of the fight, the momentum was now definitely behind the Allies.

January

The crew of a Short Sunderland flying boat drop anchor off Iceland. Patrols from Iceland had narrowed the mid-Atlantic gap, but not closed it.

Messerschmitt Bf 109 fighters captured by Soviet forces at Chir railway station as they advanced along the Middle Don sector.

A railway switch point in North Africa after having been attacked by RAF aircraft. The wreckage scattered about is from an Axis ammunition train that was caught in the attack.

Aerial transport played a role on both sides of the Tunisian campaign. Above can be seen a German gun crew with an 88-mm gun flown over from Italy. Below can be seen an RAF Lockheed Hudson transport on a captured airfield with a Hawker Hurricane fighter in the foreground.

A Boeing B-17 Flying Fortress taking off from a USAAF air base in East Anglia, silhouetted against the setting sun. The photograph below shows a daylight raid against Lille in northern France, with bombs exploding among the buildings of the ateliers de Hellemmes railway works on 13 January 1943.

Above: The wreckage of a Junkers Ju 88 shot down in a raid against London on the night of 17/18 January.

Right: Looking through the wreckage of a school in Lewisham, south London, for survivors, following a German daylight air raid on 21 January.

An RAF Lancaster crew after returning from a raid against Berlin on the night of 16/17 January. The wireless operator (second from the right) is holding a box containing pigeons that could be used to send messages.

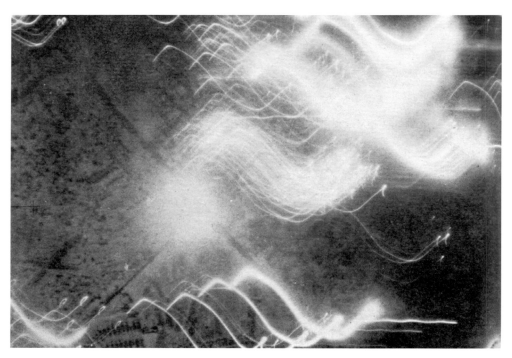

The Marienfelde district of Berlin during an RAF attack on the night of 17/18 January. The glow to the left of the centre of the photograph is over the Daimler-Benz factory.

Loading a Handley-Page Hampden with parachute bombs. These were blast weapons, designed to explode above the ground at roof level, and were capable of destroying houses over a wide area and blowing in windows further away.

A scene from the Empire Central Flying School at RAF Hullavington, near Chippenham, Wiltshire. An Australian wing commander is demonstrating, using a model aircraft and a wind tunnel, the effects of air currents for the students.

Above left: Bomb damage at the French Atlantic port of Lorient, a base for two flotillas of the German U-boat force. During the war Lorient would be hit by almost 4,000 tons of bombs, which nearly flattened the town without destroying the U-boat pens that were the raids' target.

Above right: An earlier raid against Atlantic U-boat pens, this time at Saint-Nazaire. The Saint-Nazaire U-boat base contained fourteen pens, including two that could be used as dry docks, and had a concrete roof that was 30 feet thick.

Opposite above: Göring receiving the salute in the Hall of Honour at the Air Ministry in Berlin. His speech on the tenth anniversary of Hitler's appointment as Chancellor was delayed by nuisance raids carried out by RAF Mosquito bombers.

Opposite below: An artist's impression of the RAF raid on Berlin on 30 January 1943, the Nazis' ten-year anniversary in power. As well as Göring's speech, the Mosquito bombers disrupted Goebbels' speech later in the day.

On the night of 30/31 January, RAF Bomber Command launched the first raid using the H2S ground-scanning radar system to help navigation. The target was Hamburg. The H2S system was fitted to aircraft of the Pathfinder force, which used incendiaries or flares to mark the target for the main force.

February

Australian troops disembarking from transport aircraft at Wau airfield in New Guinea in February 1943, when Australian forces were defending the airfield against Japanese attacks.

RAF ground crew in Algeria preparing what appears to be a Bristol Blenheim bomber for a mission.

A B-17 raid in progress against El Aouina airfield outside Tunis.

On 8 February, the Chindits, a
British force trained to carry out
long-range penetration missions
behind the Japanese lines, began
their first incursion into occupied
Burma. Their leader, Brigadier
Orde Wingate, can be seen on the
right-hand side in the photograph to
the right. In the photograph below
can be seen one of the RAF signal
units that accompanied the Chindits
to call in supply flights or close air
support missions.

The Commander in Chief Home Forces, General Sir Bernard Paget, inspecting airborne troops in Southern Command (based at Tidworth barracks, Wiltshire). In the background is a Horsa glider.

Japanese prisoners from the Solomon Islands disembarking under guard from a USAAF transport aircraft. The men in darker clothing are airmen in flying kit; the others are ground troops.

The Royal Navy aircraft carrier HMS *Indomitable*, which returned to the Mediterranean in February 1943 after undergoing repairs in the US, having been hit by several 500-kg bombs while escorting a Malta convoy in July and August 1942.

The flight deck of HMS *Indomitable*, including the superstructure and a Supermarine Seafire fighter.

Two photographs from the Allied daylight bombing offensive over occupied Europe, taken on separate raids on the same day – 13 February. Above, we see bombs dropped by American B-24 Liberator bombers on the Trystian Lock in Dunkirk, a sea lock leading into the town's docks. Below, an American-made Lockheed Ventura of RAF Bomber Command flies over Ijmuiden in the Netherlands; the target of the attack, the Royal Dutch Blast Furnaces and Steel Works, can be seen bottom left.

The build-up of the US Eighth Air Force in Britain continued. In this photograph, a group of B-24 Liberator bombers is on a training flight over the British countryside.

The control room of one of the airfields in the east of England used by the American bomber crews.

A photograph from a raid by US bombers on the U-boat pens in the French Atlantic coast port of Saint-Nazaire on 16 February. The U-boat pens were a key target for the bombers attempting to disrupt the German submarine offensive.

Aerial reconnaissance showing damage in the port of Wilhelmshaven on 11 February. It was estimated that about 150 acres of the city were destroyed in the raid.

Above: Soviet anti-aircraft gunners cheering as they hit a German aircraft. There was heavy fighting to the south of the Eastern Front, around the city of Kharkov, in February 1943.

Right: A map showing the front line on the Eastern Front around Kharkov and Rostov on 16 February.

Smoke rising from a 7,000-ton Japanese supply ship hit by American aircraft in the Bay of Bengal, off Rangoon, on 27 February.

March

Nazi Propaganda Minister Joseph Goebbels stands between two Catholic priests in this slightly blurry photograph, inspecting the damage to St Hedwig's church in Berlin following an air raid on the city on 1 March.

A Spitfire stands, ready to take off, on a forward desert airfield. The runway has been made of Somerfeld track, made of wire netting and designed to provide a temporary surface that aircraft could use without having to build a permanent runway.

Wings for Victory Week was launched in a ceremony with an Avro Lancaster on a platform at London's Trafalgar Square on 6 March. Wings for Victory Week was a campaign in which communities would aim to raise the funds needed to pay for bomber aircraft for the RAF.

Lines of Soviet warplanes bought using funds donated by collective farms in the Gorky and Chkalov regions on the River Volga east of Moscow.

Soviet aircrew on an airfield on the Caucasus Front in the south of the Soviet Union study a map before take-off. In the foreground two bombs can be seen hanging from the wing of one of the aircraft while two ground crew fill belts of machine-gun ammunition.

On the night of 3/4 March, two forces of German raiders mounted an attack against London, dropping their bombs on the suburbs.

Bombs falling during a raid by B-17 Flying Fortresses on Palermo docks, Sicily, on 1 March 1943. The remaining Axis forces in North Africa were supplied from Sicily.

Preparing a casualty on a stretcher before he is loaded onto a Lockheed Lodestar air ambulance for transport to a hospital behind the lines.

Sir Stafford Cripps, the Minister of Aircraft Production, talking to a female pilot from the Air Transport Auxiliary. The ATA was responsible for ferrying aircraft between airfields and factories and maintenance and repair facilities.

A Royal Canadian Air Force Halifax bomber crew walk away from their aircraft. Originally, Canadian pilots operated under RAF command, but in 1943 the RCAF organised its own separate bomber and fighter groups under Canadian command.

Above: Two Handley Page Hampden bombers converted for minelaying duties on their way to drop their mines in German-controlled waters.

Right: The flight engineer on board a Short Sunderland flying boat. On long missions over the open ocean, the flight engineer, responsible for the aircraft's engines and other mechanical systems while in flight, was vital.

A flight of Mustang fighters of the RAF's Army Co-operation Command. Although the Mustang won fame as an escort fighter for the bombers of the US Eighth Air Force, they were first sold to the RAF under Lend-Lease. The poor high-altitude performance shown by the Mustang at first led to its use by Army Co-operation Command for ground-attack missions.

The pilot of an Army Co-operation Command Mustang is being briefed for an operation in this photograph. Note the models and photographs of different types of tanks in the room; it was vital for pilots to know they were attacking the correct target.

Pilots of a squadron of Westland Whirlwinds, with two of their aircraft in the background. The Whirlwind was introduced in June 1940, but despite successful use in ground attack missions, it would be withdrawn later in 1943, to be replaced by the Bristol Beaufighter.

Two RAF armourers load drums of ammunition for the 20-mm nose-mounted cannon of a Westland Whirlwind. The Whirlwind could also carry 250-lb or 500-lb bombs.

A fixed cycle used for recording the amount of energy a pilot would expend in high-altitude flying. The dangers of fighters and flak meant that air forces became very interested in high-altitude flight and its effects on pilots and other aircrew.

April

Bombs exploding during a low-level daylight raid by Mosquito bombers against railway workshops at Trier on the Rhine on 1 April. One of the aircraft can be seen to the top right of the photograph.

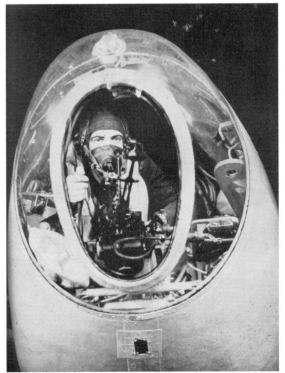

Above: Another low-level raid by RAF Mosquitoes, this time against railway workshops at Namur in Belgium on 3 April.

Left: The bomb aimer peers out through the nose of a Mosquito bomber, his thumb poised on the bomb release button.

On 18 April, a large number of German transport aircraft were shot down over the Mediterranean on their way to pick up German troops isolated by the Allied campaign in what became known as the Palm Sunday Massacre. The image above shows a damaged Junkers Ju 90 on an airfield in Tunisia. In the lower image, pilots wander back from the flight line of an advanced RAF fighter base in Tunisia towards the tents where the squadron was based.

A spectacular before and after photograph showing a bombing raid on a convoy off Bizerta on the coast of North Africa. The ship that was hit in the bottom photograph was presumably carrying a load of ammunition.

On 18 April, Admiral Isoroku
Yamamoto (right) was shot down by
American P-38 fighters (seen above)
over the island of Bougainville while
travelling on an inspection tour.

Left: Bombs can be seen falling from a B-17 of the USAAF onto the Italian cruiser *Trieste*, top right, moored in the naval base of La Maddalena on the northern coast of Sardinia on 10 April.

Below: Another photograph from the same raid. The stern and bow of the heavy cruiser *Gorizia* can just be seen through the smoke as bombs explode around her.

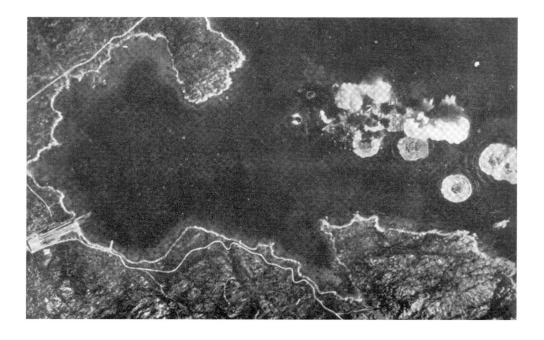

Two photographs taken following the RAF bombing raid against Stuttgart on the night of 14/15 April. The upper photograph shows a crew gathered around the wheel of their aircraft, while the lower photograph shows another crew gathered around a WAAF, reporting on how the raid went. Aircrews would report on the accuracy of the bombing, whether they attacked the main target or a secondary one, and enemy flak and night-fighter defences.

An RAF Hurricane fighter on patrol over Bengal in the east of India, on watch for Japanese aircraft.

A Japanese destroyer on fire and sinking in the Bismarck Sea, having been hit by bombs from Allied aircraft.

Above left: Japanese prisoners under guard being flown out of the Solomon Islands to the American South Pacific HQ.

Above right: American ground crew preparing bombs on an airfield on a South Pacific airfield, with a B-17 Flying Fortress in the background.

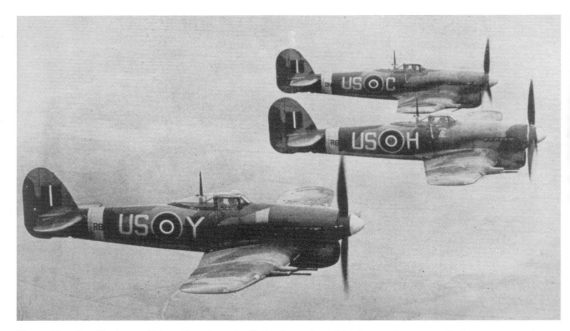

Three Hawker Typhoon fighter bombers in flight. Introduced in September 1941, in late 1942 and 1943 Typhoons were first equipped with the bombs and ground attack rockets for which they would gain their reputation.

May

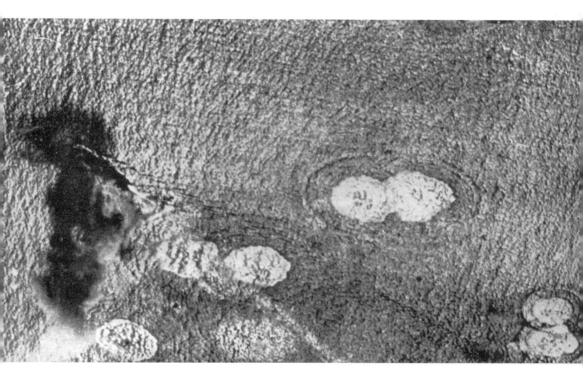

A Japanese transport under attack from Allied bombers in the Pacific. Marks can be seen in the water on either side of the wake, showing where earlier attacks had missed, but the vessel appears to have been on fire when the photograph was taken.

Above left: American-made Douglas DB-7 Boston III bombers supplied to the Soviet Air Force under the Lend-Lease Agreement in action.

Above right: A group of Soviet aircrew walking away from their aircraft after returning from an air raid against Tilsit in East Prussia. Now known as Sovetsk, Tilsit is part of Russia's Kaliningrad Oblast.

Opposite: The P-47 Thunderbolt was used as both a fighter-bomber in support of Allied troops on the ground and as an escort fighter for the B-17 and B-24 bombers attacking targets in Germany and occupied Europe.

On the night of 16/17 May, Lancaster bombers of 617 Squadron launched Operation Chastise, attacking the Möhne, Eder and Sorpe dams using Barnes Wallis's bouncing bombs, code-named Upkeep. This is an artist's impression of the operation.

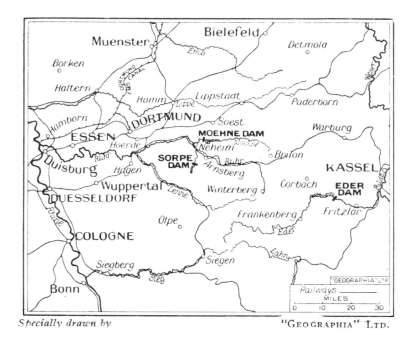

Specially drawn by   "GEOGRAPHIA" LTD.

The Möhne, Eder and Sorpe dams controlled supplies of water in the Ruhr region in western Germany. This was not just used as drinking water but also for generating hydroelectricity, making steel and maintaining the water level in the area's canals.

Right: The breach in the Möhne Dam, with water pouring through.

Below: Water pouring through one of the two breaches in the wall of the Eder Dam.

Flooding in the Ruhr Valley caused by the breaches in the dams. German authorities estimated some 1,600 people died as a result of the raid.

One of the crews from the Dambusters mission being debriefed on their return to Britain. Air Chief Marshal Sir Arthur 'Bomber' Harris, the controversial chief of Bomber Command, is standing to the left.

Wing-Commander Guy Gibson, commander of 617 Squadron and leader of the Dambusters raid, can be seen on the right of this photograph.

A raid on an Axis convoy of six supply ships and eight escorts off the coast of the Netherlands carried out by Bristol Beaufighters. Two of the supply ships were claimed as hit and set alight, while a further three were claimed damaged.

A closer view of a Bristol Beaufighter of RAF Coastal Command, carrying a torpedo. The openings for two of the aircraft's four cannon can be seen. As well as serving with Coastal Command, Beaufighters served as night fighters and ground attack aircraft.

On 29 May, the industrial town of Wuppertal was attacked by RAF Bomber Command, causing heavy civilian casualties. This photograph shows a Lancaster bomber silhouetted against the light coming up from the fires and Wuppertal's defences, as well as by the photographic flash bomb seen to the right.

On 28 May, the king visited 617 Squadron's base at RAF Scampton in Lincolnshire. He is seen here with Air Vice Marshal Ralph Cochrane, commander of 5 Group, far left, and Guy Gibson, second from left.

June

A tanker, part of a transatlantic convoy, is seen out of the window of a B-24 Liberator of Coastal Command. Liberators, with their extremely long range, played a major role in narrowing the gap in the mid-Atlantic, where U-boats could operate out of range of Allied aircraft.

Above: The city centre of Düsseldorf following a major bombing raid on 11 June. It was estimated that some 1,500 acres of the city centre were destroyed, with the main railway station, the municipal power station, the main post office, the gasworks and many factories and industrial facilities in the area affected.

Left: The city of Münster following an air raid on 11 June. Fires can still be seen burning in an area of badly damaged warehouses and other commercial property (top centre), while one of the city's gas holders has also been badly damaged (left centre) and the goods station has been severely hit (bottom).

The island of Pantellaria was bombed heavily before its garrison commander surrendered to the Allies on 11 June. The image to the right shows bombs exploding along the island's waterfront, while the image below shows smoke drifting up from the island after a raid just hours before the island's surrender.

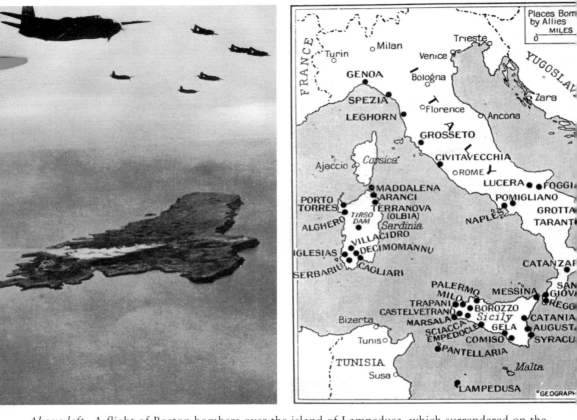

Above left: A flight of Boston bombers over the island of Lampedusa, which surrendered on the evening of 12 June, the day after the surrender of Pantellaria. Like Pantellaria, Lampedusa was bombarded by warships and aircraft prior to its surrender.

Above right: Pantellaria and Lampedusa can be seen in the Mediterranean south of Sicily.

Thanks to his involvement in planning the Pearl Harbor attack, Admiral Yamamoto became a figure of hate in the United States. The attack on his transport plane was considered to be vengeance for Pearl Harbor.

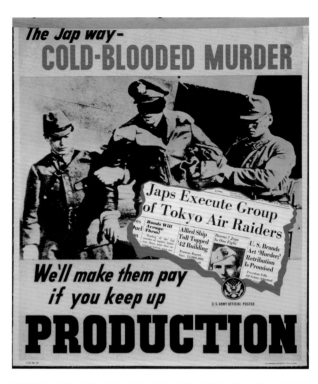

This poster appeared in 1943 after the reported execution of three of the Doolittle raiders in Shanghai at the end of 1942 for strafing Japanese civilians.

Liberty For All: an appeal to support the US Navy and its aircraft carriers in the Pacific.

A poster calling on patriotic American women to join the WAC, the Women's Army Corps. Members of the WAC worked in support roles on USAAF bases in Britain, starting in 1943.

Left: Another way in which women could help the war effort was by working in one of the factories across the US, which turned out almost endless lines of aircraft and other war materiel.

Below: An appeal for war bonds to finance the cost of buying all the weapons needed to fight a modern war.

An aircrew member of the US Eighth Air Force on the ground at a base somewhere in East Anglia.

B-17G *Miss Fury*.

Opposite above: This B-17, *Cock o' the Walk*, served with the 388th Bomb Group, which was stationed at RAF Knettishall in Suffolk.

Opposite below: B-17 *Sweet and Lovely* was assigned to the 482nd Bomb Group at Alconbury in Cambridgeshire in August 1943. It survived the war and was scrapped in the US.

Above: An aircrew member of the US Eighth Air Force on the ground at a base somewhere in East Anglia.

Opposite: B-17 *Tom Paine* was based at Knettishall in Suffolk, arriving in September 1943, and was scrapped after a crash landing in Norfolk, when returning from a mission in April 1944.

The bombardier in the nose of a B-17G, showing the chin turret which was developed to counter frontal attacks from German fighters.

A P-47 Thunderbolt sitting on the tarmac. On long missions, Thunderbolts could only escort the bombers so far and then meet them on the way back. This Thunderbolt carries a drop tank to improve range.

A B-17 returning to its base at the end of a mission.

Opposite: A group of Messerschmitt Bf 110 pilots are briefed in the open air on their next mission. Bf 110s were used to intercept the American bombers. Equipped with radar, they also served as night fighters, intercepting the aircraft of RAF Bomber Command.

In these two photographs, Mussolini is seen walking towards the Fieseler Storch light aircraft brought by the paratroopers and SS troops who rescued him from a mountaintop ski resort where he was being held under arrest. In the lower photograph, the aircraft is seen taking off, heading for Rome.

In December, a force of Ju 88s of Luftflotte 2 carried out a successful raid against shipping in Bari harbour, showing the Luftwaffe was still a force to be reckoned with.

'United we are strong, United we will win.' An Allied propaganda poster which alludes to the strength of the Allied manufacturing base, key in churning out weapons like aircraft.

Above: A photograph taken during an air raid on the Sicilian city of Messina on 18 June. The bombs dropped by the USAAF's B-17s can be seen exploding around the city administration building and the slips for the ferries that connect Sicily with Calabria on the Italian mainland. Air raids were carried out against both Sicily and Sardinia to conceal the Allies' next step after the end of the fighting in North Africa.

Right: A Lockheed Ventura bomber over Vlissingen in the Netherlands, as part of a raid on shipyards and oil storage tanks there on 24 June. By the summer of 1943 the Ventura, Lockheed's development of the Hudson, was being phased out of use as a bomber, being neither suitable for the purpose nor popular with crews.

Two rather eerie photographs taken during night raids by RAF Bomber Command on targets in Germany. The upper photograph shows what look to be searchlights and anti-aircraft fire over Lake Constance, just to the north of the Alps, during a raid on a factory at Friedrichshafen on 20 June. The lower photograph shows a weaving pattern of searchlight beams from a raid on Berlin.

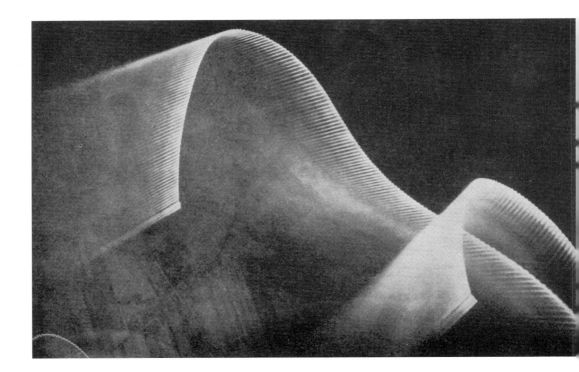

As an alternative to transporting aircraft to the Middle East on convoys through the dangerous Mediterranean, or on the long route around the coast of Africa and through the Red Sea, they could be flown the 6,000 miles across Africa. The top image shows the fuselage, tail unit and wings of a Hurricane being removed from their packing crates and carried by hand to an assembly bay at an airfield in West Africa. The lower image shows a fuel stop in the desert.

Attacks by the Allied air forces against the industrial area of the Ruhr Valley continued into the end of June, leading to the evacuation of a great many civilians from the area. This photograph shows a USAAF B-17 over the Buna rubber works at Hüls in the Ruhr.

Another image of the continuing bomber offensive against the Ruhr: this photograph shows damage to a steel works in Bochum following an attack by RAF Bomber Command, with the numbers marking the finishing section (1), the steel furnaces (2), the rolling mill (3) and the offices (4).

At the end of June, a glider carrying a ton and a half of supplies was towed by an aircraft across the Atlantic from Montreal to Britain. The upper image shows the glider and its towing aircraft in flight while the lower image is a closer view of the American-made Hadrian glider, named *Voo-Doo*.

This photograph shows a freighter on its side, blocking the entrance to Levkas harbour, Greece, following an attack by RAF Beaufighter aircraft on 27 June.

July

On 28 June
and 3 July, RAF
Bomber Command
returned to
Cologne.
Although the
original caption
to this aerial
reconnaissance
photograph
points out that
the cathedral (in
the top left of the
picture) suffered
'only very slightly',
the damage caused
by bombing to the
rest of the city can
be seen in the large
number of roofless
houses.

Two more photographs of the bombing raid on Cologne on 3 July. The upper photograph shows the Klockner Humboldt-Deutz works, which was targeted because diesel engines for submarines were manufactured there, while the bottom photograph shows the marshalling yards and chemical factory in the district of Kalk on the east bank of the Rhine.

On 10 July, Operation Husky, the invasion of Sicily, began. Allied airborne troops played a major role in the invasion, although many of the paratroopers and glider infantry were scattered by high winds, and some landed in the sea.

Specially drawn by   "GEOGRAPHIA" LTD.

Above: A map of Sicily. British paratroopers seized a bridge just south of Syracuse to allow British troops to move inland from the landing beaches.

Left: General Montgomery addresses men of the 4th Parachute Brigade prior to the invasion of Sicily. Due to a lack of transport, the brigade was landed by sea rather than from the air.

Above: Paratroopers defended
Sicily as well. German paratroopers,
Fallschirmjäger, taken prisoner by
Allied troops, are seen marching away
from the front line.

Right: B-25 Mitchell bombers of the
USAAF mounting a low-level attack on
the road network in Sicily in an attempt
to hold up the movements of German
and Italian troops.

Left: On 19 July, the Allies bombed Rome for the first time, when B-17s and B-24s of the USAAF attacked targets such as munitions factories, government buildings and, as in this photograph, marshalling yards.

Below: A map of the centre of Rome, showing the military targets (marshalling yards and the various ministries) in relation to the cultural sites of the city.

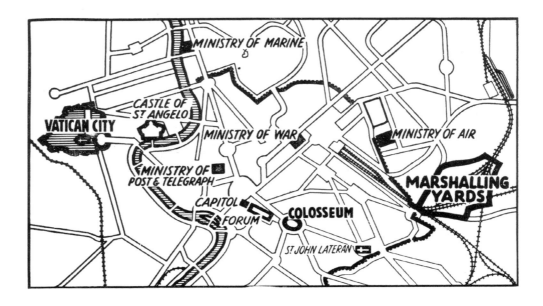

Between 1 a.m. and 2 a.m. on 24 July, RAF bombers dropped more than 2,000 tons of bombs on Hamburg, a mixture of 4,000-lb 'Cookies' and incendiaries designed to create a firestorm in the city. This was the start of Operation Gomorrah, a bombing campaign against Hamburg. Attacks by both the RAF and the USAAF continued through the last week of July, the final raid being mounted on 2/3 August. This photograph shows damage in the St Georg area of Hamburg, on the Outer Alster lake.

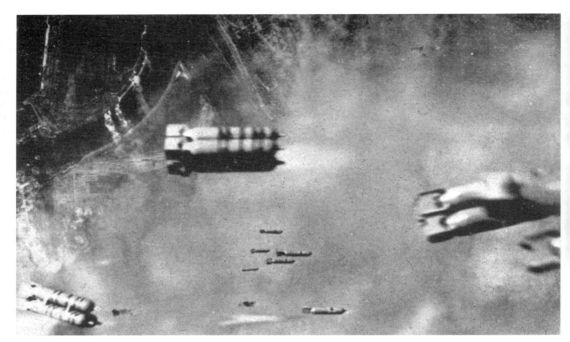

On 26 July, the US Eighth Air Force also attacked the port city of Hamburg as part of Operation Gomorrah. The upper photograph shows clusters of incendiary bombs falling on one of Hamburg's U-boat construction yards, while the lower photograph shows bombs bursting on a shipyard in the city as a pall of smoke from the RAF raid two nights previously drifts across the image.

Above left: An air attack against a railway in Burma. Bombs can be seen exploding over and around the line, while there appears to be timber scattered on the ground below the railway in the lower part of the image.

Above right: A cloud of smoke rises up from the city of Minbu, on the Irrawaddy River in Burma. Minbu was attacked by American aircraft, which dropped some 20 tons of bombs.

Members of the first contingent of the WAAC, the Women's Army Auxiliary Corps, to arrive in Britain to serve with the Eighth Air Force, some 650 strong, march into their camp.

August

B-24 Liberator bombers. On 1 August, a force of B-24s flying from bases in North
Africa attacked the oil refineries around the Romanian city of Ploesti in one of the
costliest missions for the USAAF in Europe during the war.

The B-24s were supposed to fly in at an extremely low level to avoid the German radar, but heavy cloud cover over the Pindus Mountains in Albania disrupted their formations. (USAF)

The classic image of the Ploesti mission: a B-24 highlighted against a plume of black smoke rising from the Astra Romana refinery. (USAF)

Left: Another image of the Astra Romana, with more B-24s coming in over the target. (USAF)

Below: A line-up of B-24s from the 376th Bombardment Group, seen at a desert airfield outside Benghazi after the Ploesti mission. (USAF)

RAF ground crew watch as a Spitfire lifts off from a Sicilian landing ground that used to be a wheat field and was rapidly converted after the crop was harvested.

The final stage of the Sicilian campaign: this map shows the front line on Sicily on 3 August.

Damage to the Tuscolano district of Rome after an air raid by American bombers on 13 August.

The Pope, Pius XII, tours the damaged districts of Rome following the raid of 13 August, giving his blessing to the crowds.

The results of an air raid on the night of 17/18 August on the research establishment at Peenemünde on Germany's Baltic coast, where Dr Werner von Braun's team were working on what would become the V-2 rocket. This was the start of Operation Crossbow, targeting the V-weapon programme.

Earlier on 17 August, bombers of the US Eighth Air Force mounted a raid deep into southern Germany, attacking the ball-bearing plant at Schweinfurt and the oil refinery and Messerschmitt Bf 109 assembly plant at Regensburg, and suffering heavy losses in the process. This photograph shows bombs exploding on the assembly plant at Regensburg.

Two photographs of Messina, the city in Sicily closest to the Italian mainland, at the end of the Sicilian campaign. The image above shows the railway station and marshalling yards, while the image below shows the city's waterfront. Both have been heavily damaged in air raids.

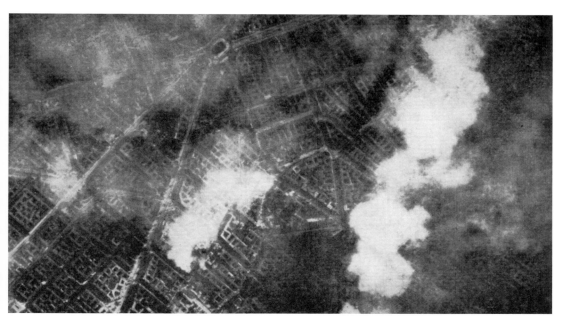

On the night of 23/24 August, more than 700 RAF bombers attacked Berlin. In the photograph above, fires can be seen burning in the centre of the city, while in the lower photograph the crew of a Short Stirling are being debriefed on their return. Stirlings were being used less and less on operations such as this, as their lower altitude meant that they were more vulnerable to defences on the ground and their crews often found themselves flying through bombs being dropped by the higher-flying Halifaxes and Lancasters.

B-17 Flying Fortresses over the German airfield at Amiens-Glisy, which was attacked on 31 August.

September

The city of Milan following an air raid; furniture from damaged properties has been stacked in the road while a bombed-out family eats in the open air.

American paratroopers landing on Lae airfield in New Guinea, protected by a billowing smokescreen. This was the first large-scale use of paratroopers in the Pacific theatre of the war, and was a textbook operation. General MacArthur watched from a circling B-17 bomber.

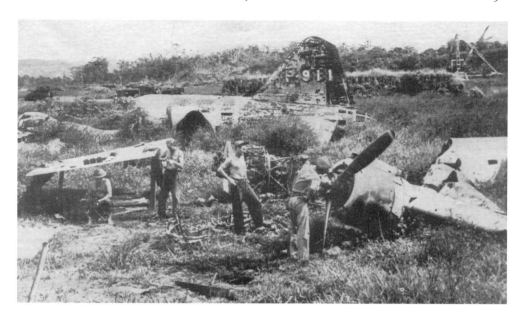

Above: American and Australian troops examining the wreckage of Japanese aircraft on the airfield at Lae in New Guinea after it was occupied by Allied troops in mid-September. Australian troops advancing overland through the jungle linked up with the American paratroopers on the airfield.

Right: Parachute bombs falling among dispersed and camouflaged Japanese aircraft on an airfield at Wewak on New Guinea.

Above: Bombs bursting around Japanese shipping in the harbour at Wewak. Two of the attacking aircraft are circled.

Opposite top: RAF Martin Baltimore bombers over the Italian mountains as they attack a German division moving up to reinforce the defences around Salerno.

Opposite bottom: On 14 September, troops of the Allied Fifth Army under the command of the American general Mark Clark landed at Salerno on the Italian mainland south of Naples. This map shows the bridgehead after a week of fighting.

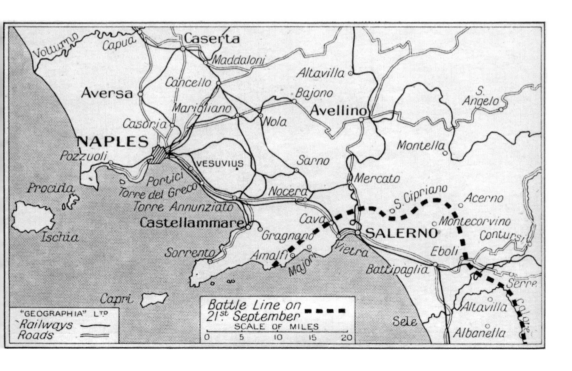

A raid by Eighth Air Force B-17s on the U-boat locks (A) and pens (B) at La Pallice, the port of La Rochelle, on the French Atlantic coast on 16 September. The bombers also attacked the dispersal area of a nearby airfield (circled).

A Stearman trainer is seen above Carlstrom Field, Arcadia, Florida, one of the American airfields to which RAF cadet pilots were sent for flight training, because the better weather meant more potential flying time.

A trainee bomber pilot is receiving his final instructions from his instructor in an Airspeed Oxford.

A mechanic putting the finishing touches to a Spitfire in the main assembly shop of a large aircraft factory. The largest Spitfire plant was the shadow factory at Castle Bromwich in the West Midlands, which had produced over 12,000 Spitfires by June 1945.

A section of the assembly line at a factory producing the Avro Lancaster heavy bomber. Nearly half of the 7,000 Lancasters made were produced at Avro's factories in Manchester and Cheshire, with 700 more produced at a shadow factory outside Leeds.

North American B-25 Marauders in action over Europe. The twin-engined Marauder was used for ground-attack missions, bombing road and rail links in Italy and the Balkans.

A B-24 Liberator setting off from Iceland for a sixteen-hour patrol over the convoys in the North Atlantic. The availability of more Liberators equipped for the patrols was a key factor in the fight against the U-boats.

The navigator of a B-24 on patrol in the Atlantic takes a sighting with his sextant. Such seemingly old-fashioned equipment was vital for navigation over the open ocean in the days before reliable electronic navigation aids.

Removed from power in July, in September Benito Mussolini was rescued from the mountaintop hotel in the Abruzzo where he was being held in a daring airborne mission by German paratroopers and SS troops led by Otto Skorzeny.

October

A B-24 Liberator flies over the port of Bastia in Corsica, the last remaining one through which the occupying German forces could leave the island, having been pushed out by Free French and Italian forces following the Italian armistice. Allied aircraft bombed the town to halt the exodus.

The airfield at Peacock Point on Japanese-occupied Wake Island following a raid by the US Navy on 5 October; the airfield was both bombed and shelled during the attack.

A wrecked Japanese Mitsubishi G4M 'Betty' bomber at Munda airfield on New Georgia Island in the Solomon Islands, east of New Guinea.

Two photographs showing RAF air attacks in Burma. In the top left image, dense black smoke rises from oil tanks hit by RAF Beaufighters; fuel supplies were a major problem for the Japanese, and securing them was one of the reasons for launching their campaigns in the Far East. The top right image shows a camouflaged steamship under attack on a Burmese river creek.

Opposite above: A B-25 Mitchell bomber attacking German artillery positions in Italy; the German guns were bombarding troops of the Fifth Army attempting to cross the Volturno River.

Opposite below: An RAF ground-attack aircraft, either a Kittyhawk or a Warhawk, is seen about to take off, with two more visible in the dust behind it. Close air support was vital as Allied troops in Italy attempted to dislodge the occupying German forces.

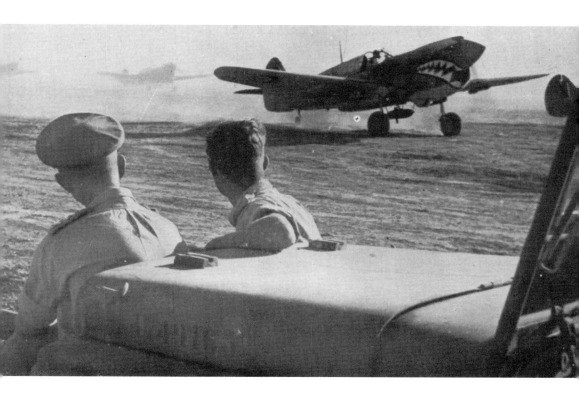

A B-17 Flying Fortress with the blazing Focke-Wulf aircraft works at Marienburg in East Prussia in the background. The US Eighth Air Force attacked the Marienburg works on 9 October as part of a plan to disrupt the German aircraft industry.

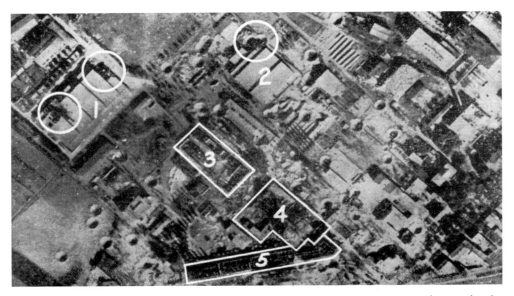

Another of the targets for the Eighth Air Force on 9 October was a components factory for the Arado aircraft company at Anklam in the north-east of Germany, near what is now the Polish border. The numbered areas mark different workshops in the factory that were damaged in the raid, including the press shop, machine shop and various sub-assembly shops.

B-17s of the Eighth Air Force flying through black bursts of anti-aircraft fire. German anti-aircraft defences were heavy and sophisticated, and proved a major worry for the bomber pilots.

A reconnaissance photograph showing the damage caused by the Eighth Air Force to the ball-bearing works at Schweinfurt in the north of what is now Bavaria on 14 October. The areas marked A to E on the photograph are individual plants, while F marks the location of the railway yards.

Left: The Italian railway network was the subject of heavy air attacks as the Allies attempted to stem the flow of supplies and reinforcements to the Axis defenders. This image shows the wreckage of a train of aircraft parts for the Luftwaffe in a marshalling yard outside Naples.

Below: A wrecked Italian Macchi C200 fighter is seen in the foreground of this wrecked hangar on Capodichino airfield near Naples, with wrecked transport aircraft in the background.

Two views of an air ambulance evacuating casualties from Sicily. The top view is an external view of a casualty on a stretcher being loaded into an air ambulance. The bottom photograph is an interior view with a casualty in the foreground. Two air ambulances, costing £10,000 each, were presented to the RAF after a collection of donations from all over the British Empire.

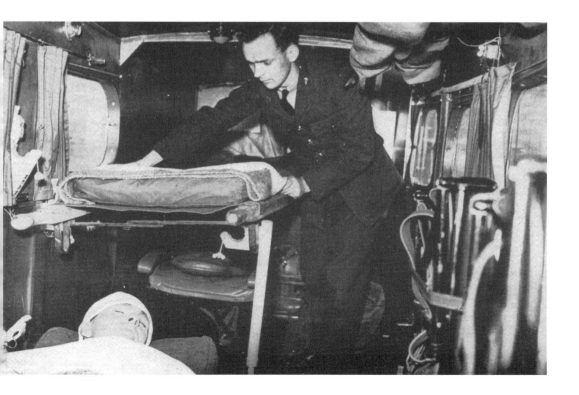

Mariendorf gasworks, Berlin. Two burnt-out gas holders can be seen at the top of the picture, along with a great deal of other damage from bombing. In November, Sir Arthur Harris and Bomber Command would launch a concerted campaign of air attacks against the Nazi capital.

B-17s flying back to North Africa over the French Riviera after attacking a railway viaduct south-west of Cannes on 31 October.

November

A B-24 Liberator of the US Fifteenth Air Force passes over the Messerschmitt assembly plant at Wiener Neustadt, south-west of Vienna, as clouds of smoke billow over the target. Flying from bases in North Africa and Italy, the Fifteenth were better able to reach targets like this than the Eighth Air Force in East Anglia.

Above: P-47 Thunderbolt
fighters on their way across
the English Channel.
When escorting fighters
did not have the range to
accompany the bombers
for the whole mission, they
would accompany them as
far as possible on the way out
and then meet the returning
bomber formations on the
way back.

Right: An RAF Spitfire sits
on an Italian airfield that has
been turned into a lake by
torrential rain.

A railway bridge near Giulianova on the Adriatic coast of Italy, damaged by a direct hit from a bomb dropped by an Allied aircraft.

Opposite: B-17 Flying Fortresses of the US Fifteenth Air Force flying over the town of Bolzano in northern Italy, en route to attack railway yards outside the town.

A line of Handley Page Halifax bombers of the Royal Australian Air Force on an airfield in the Mediterranean.

A map showing the range of targets accessible to Allied aircraft operating from Foggia, north and east of Naples, including Athens, Belgrade, western Romania, Budapest, Vienna and Toulon.

Above: The spectacular pattern of anti-aircraft gunfire over Naples mixed with the light of flares dropped by German aircraft to illuminate their targets as they launched an air attack on the city.

Right: Sailors on board a US Navy aircraft carrier prepare bundles of incendiary bombs prior to a raid on Tarawa in the Gilbert Islands in the Pacific. Tarawa was bombed heavily by American aircraft prior to the landing on the island by the US Marines on 20 November.

Above: In November, the so-called Battle for Berlin, a concerted series of air attacks on the German capital, began. This photograph shows senior officers of one of Bomber Command's groups in the operations room, planning an attack.

Left: Aircrew from a Mosquito squadron stand by their aircraft under a bright moon prior to take-off. Mosquitoes would carry out small raids against Berlin as part of the bombing campaign. From late 1943, Mosquito squadrons were formed into the Light Night Strike Force, and were used both for small 'nuisance raids' and as pathfinders for the heavy bombers.

Above: Ground crew loading a 4,000-lb bomb into the bomb bay of a Lancaster prior to the heavy air raid against Berlin on the night of 22/23 November.

Right: The bomb aimer of a Lancaster about to press the release button. Bomb aimers would have to look for the special coloured target markers dropped ahead of the main bomber force by the pathfinders to ensure they dropped their bombs in the right place.

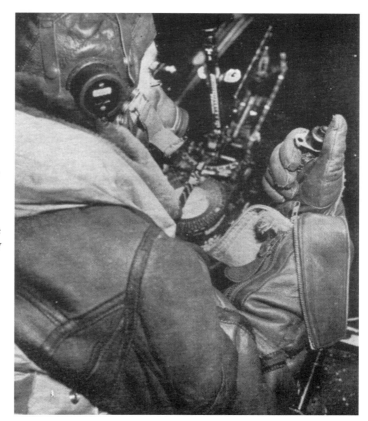

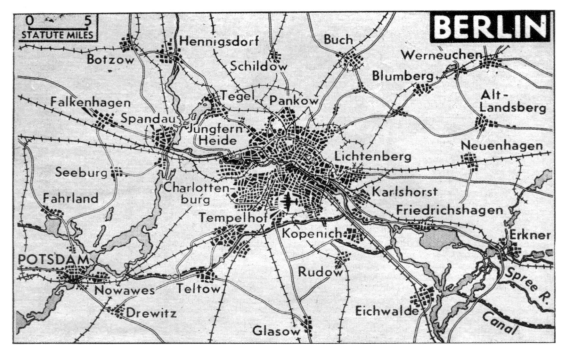

Berlin and the surrounding districts. The raid of 22/23 November caused extensive damage to the residential districts to the west of the city, including Charlottenburg and Spandau.

The debriefing of one of the Lancaster crews after their return from the Berlin raid.

The operational headquarters of a Luftwaffe unit somewhere on the Eastern Front. In November the Red Army were fighting a successful offensive in the Ukraine, retaking Kiev on the anniversary of the Russian Revolution in 1917.

Petrol carried in what look to be bomb casings is unloaded from a German transport aircraft in northern Italy. The Germans fought hard to slow the Allied advance north through Italy.

A B-17 of the RAF lands on the Azores islands in the Atlantic, west of the Iberian Peninsula. In August, Portugal had granted the Allies use of the Azores for air and naval bases, citing the Anglo-Portuguese treaty of 1373. In November, more submarines than Allied shipping had been destroyed.

December

The effects of the sustained bombing campaign against Berlin can be seen in this photograph of a street in the Wittenberg district of the city. Firestorms had been ignited by the raids of 22/23 November, destroying large areas of housing.

Above: A vivid artist's impression of an attack by RAF Typhoon fighters against a formation of Dornier 217 bombers over the Netherlands. Of the fourteen Dorniers, the RAF pilots claimed to have shot down eleven.

Left: Loading a 500-lb bomb under the wing of a Typhoon. By the end of 1943, Typhoon squadrons were the backbone of the RAF's ground attack force in Europe.

Bombs bursting on a road junction to the north of Romagnoli in an air attack intended to disrupt communications for the German forces in Italy.

Ground crew working hard to release a Spitfire from the mud on an Italian airfield.

RAF Baltimore bombers on their way to attack artillery positions near Lanciano, on the Adriatic coast of Italy, almost opposite Rome. The German defenders in Italy used artillery very effectively to slow the Allied advance.

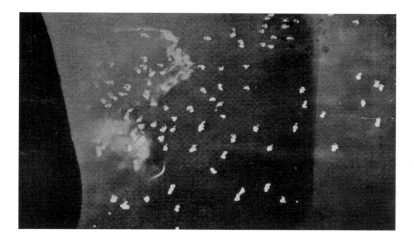

Top and middle: Two photographs from an attack made by the US Eighth Air Force against the city of Bremen on 20 December. The upper photograph was taken from the rear of a B-24 Liberator (part of the tail fin can be seen to the left) and shows anti-aircraft fire exploding. The lower photograph shows B-17s, condensation trailing behind them, dropping their bombs on Bremen.

American mechanics from a mobile repair unit are hard at work on this B-17, named *Stella*, after it sustained heavy damage on a mission and had to make a forced landing at its base in Britain.

Above left: A Canadian woman at work at the Fairchild aircraft factory in Montreal, kneeling in the cockpit of a Bolingbroke, a Canadian variant of the Bristol Blenheim built up until 1943.

Above right: A crew mans a Bofors anti-aircraft gun on Fair Isle off the north coast of Scotland.

Three members of the ATS in a control room for plotting the tracks of enemy aircraft over London and feeding the information to the anti-aircraft gunners.

Top and middle: Two photographs showing a B-24 Liberator attacking a U-boat in the Atlantic. The upper image shows the Liberator sweeping over the submarine, while the lower image shows a near hit with a depth charge.

HMS *Battler*, one of the escort carriers that could provide air cover for convoys all the way across the Atlantic. Built in the US as a merchant ship, she entered service as an aircraft carrier with the Royal Navy in late 1942.

Above: One of the aircraft types that the *Battler* could carry was the American-made Vought Corsair seen here.

Left: Ground crew stand beside a B-17G, which featured a remote-controlled chin turret (seen here) to defend against head-on attack by enemy fighters. The final production model of the Flying Fortress, the B-17G, came into service in the second half of 1943, and more than 8,000 were made.